Where the Trout Are All as Long as Your Leg

BOOKS BY JOHN GIERACH

FLY-FISHING THE HIGH COUNTRY

TROUT BUM

THE VIEW FROM RAT LAKE

FLY-FISHING SMALL STREAMS

SEX, DEATH, AND FLY-FISHING

WHERE THE TROUT ARE ALL
AS LONG AS YOUR LEG

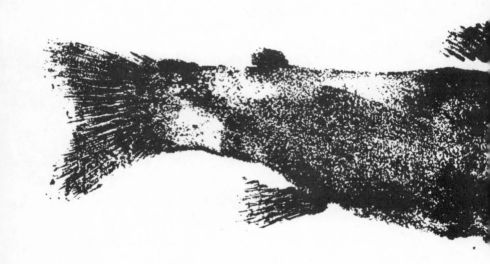

Where the Trout Are All

LYONS & BURFORD, PUBLISHERS

JOHN GIERACH

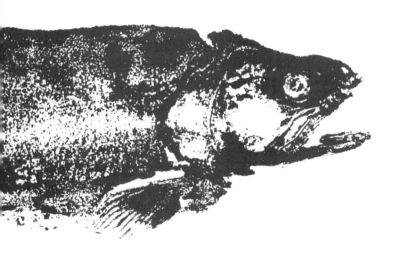

as Long as Your Leg

Library of Congress Cataloging-in-Publication Data

Gierach, John, 1946–
    Where the trout are all as long as your leg / John Gierach.
        p.   cm.
    ISBN 1-55821-098-9 : $14.95
    1. Trout fishing—United States. 2. Fly fishing—United
States. 3. Gierach, John, 1946–   . I. Title.
SH688.U6G54   1991
799.1'755—dc20   90-19308
                                                                              CIP

Printed in the United States of America

10   9   8   7   6   5   4

Text design by Liz Driesbach

Gyotaku (pronounced something like "jo-taku") is an ancient Japanese art form in which prints are made by inking a fish and pressing rice paper on it. In Japanese, "gyo" means "fish" and "taku" means "print" or "rubbing." It's harder than it sounds.

Gyotaku has been practiced in Japan for about six centuries. Like so much of Japanese culture before World War Two, it probably originated in China. Some consider it an art form while others see it as just a neat way to record a catch. Traditionally, the species of fish, where it was caught, and the name of the fisherman are written on the print.

I made the prints used in this book and on the dust jacket in Colorado in the summer of 1990.

—*JOHN GIERACH*

Where the Trout Are All as Long as Your Leg

The secret places are the soul of fishing. You know, as in, "Listen, it's a long drive, but I know this place where . . ." You can fill in the blank from what you've heard for yourself in the past: "Where the trout are all as long as your leg," "Where only the rancher and I have keys to the gate," "Where no one ever fishes."

We've all heard it, and it never fails to make the hair stand up on our arms. Sure, we've been around some and we know about fishing. We know that it's out of the bag now, that it's a growth industry over-populated with participants and gizmos. But we also know that there are hidden places out there somewhere—remote, private, camouflaged in some way, or all of the above—where it still hasn't changed. This is the hopeful mythology of the sport that

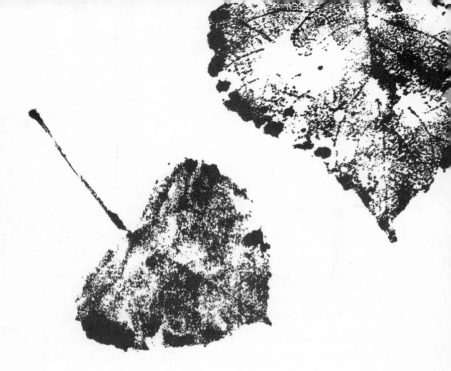

we all cling to, but it also happens to be absolutely true. You can't dismiss us as romantics because we've seen the proof.

A secret spot has only one advantage: for one reason or another, few fishermen get on it, so it isn't pounded much. It may be a private spring creek with armed guards where there are huge browns and lots of them, or it may just be an unknown beaver pond where a handful of brook trout have grown to a whopping eleven inches. In either case, it's a spot that, by the simple virtue of being left more or less alone, has reached its full potential.

4

Fishing secret spots can be as different from fishing in general as small settlements are from big cities. Chances are you're in a state that's known for its fishing, but, acting on a tip, you're now in a part of it that you've never seen or heard much about. The main industry here is agriculture, which doesn't make an area famous in the same way sport does. There are lots of farmers on the roads, but few other fishermen, which makes the place seem more vacant than it really is.

You drive into town looking for a room (Main Street may have a bait joint, but no Orvis shop) and find the backwater motel with peeling paint that will be nice and cheap. This is a secondary tourist route, at best. If the name of the town is, say, Duck Creek, then the motel will be the Duck Inn—something cute from the 1950s.

The guy who rents you the room seems dazed and a little unsure of his duties. It's an off-season weekday, so maybe he's not the regular desk clerk. It becomes obvious that he is unable to make change, so, after an awkward pause, you do it for him. He gives you a look, wondering if you've screwed him, but he can't tell for sure. After another pause, he lets it go and gives you the key.

In a city, this poor guy would be eaten alive—he'd be carrying brown paper luggage and sleeping in a doorway—but in this part of the world he gets a break. He has what passes for a job and, presumably, a dry place to sleep. You're a little sorry for him, but not like you'd be for a genuine street person. Suddenly you begin to feel very good about tomorrow's fishing because you know that guys like this are like big, easy trout: if they can live where it's quiet, uncrowded and slow-paced, they can survive.

T W O

One of the earliest memories I have that amounts to a fishing story has to do with a secret spot. Since this is an old recollection from childhood, it's a little out of focus in places, but something very much like this happened.

I guess I was about five years old, and the Second World War hadn't been over for much

6

longer than that. We lived in a big square brick house in a little town in Illinois—my older sister, mother, father, grandmother, and I. We were a standard postwar extended family unit: three generations in one house, which was owned and largely run by the oldest, grayest member.

The first President I remember was Eisenhower—Ike, a kindly, bald man who fished a lot—and the first thing I remember clearly about him is when he got caught lying about the U-2 spy-plane incident. People were genuinely scandalized. Imagine, an elected official lying! I'm only forty-three years old now, but those seem like awfully remote times.

At the end of the street our house was on—a thirty-second bike ride away—was the woods, and a few hundred yards back in there you'd come to the creek. It wasn't much of a creek, but I didn't know that then. It was the only one I'd ever seen.

This was the Forest Preserve, a sprawling hardwood boondocks that surrounded the town on all but the one side where the corn fields were. It was state-owned, but the state was not much in evidence. There were no signs telling you what you couldn't do in there, and so, by

7

implication at least, you could do what you pleased. There were no marked trails or outhouses, and there were no official "access points" either. You just stepped into the trees wherever you felt like it. This was just The Woods, and we kids were in there all the time.

In the summer we were mostly down along the creek fishing, that is, doing what kids do when they say they're fishing. We carried sticks, string, and hooks, and, based on some old family photos, we even got into real cane poles at some point, but we caught more frogs and turtles than catfish, and we usually caught them by hand between games of Cowboys and Indians.

I remember overhearing some adult saying that I was growing up "like a wild Indian." I took it as a compliment.

There were rules, of course. You could go into the woods, but you couldn't go past the dead tree at the bottom of the hill and you couldn't cross the creek. The big people laid down these laws, but they didn't bother to give us any good reasons for them, so we decided they were arbitrary and tended to flirt with the boundaries. Once we were down in the woods, it seemed like all bets were off.

To avoid getting caught, we developed a minimalist, two-syllable style of testimony:

"Where have you been?"

"The Woods."

"How did you get so dirty?"

"Fell down."

"What were you doing?"

"Nothin'."

"Well, did you boys have fun?"

"I guess."

The fun business involved some ticklish theology. Grandma was a sweet old lady, but she had a stern side, and she was also deeply religious. She may even have qualified as a mystic because she spoke with—that is, *conversed with*—The Lord on a daily basis. The two of them pretty much agreed on everything, including the idea that fun was sinful, or maybe that certain *kinds* of fun were sinful, or maybe it was too much fun. Something like that. I was never clear on the concept then and still don't entirely understand it.

So the wisest course of action with the adults was to downplay enthusiasm, avoid the particulars, and live a kind of secret life. What were we doing at the creek all afternoon?

"Nothin'," which is to say, none of your business.

If you think children don't have that kind of self-respect, you have just forgotten.

One day we heard from some big kids that there was a secret place to fish way down the creek. Way down: miles and miles, they said. We listened to this with some interest, since 10 none of us had ever caught a fish longer than six inches and the problem had to be with where we were fishing, right? Even today that's often the problem.

There were huge catfish down there that they, of course, caught all the time and that no one else knew about. We got this in the taunting way you got everything from the big kids: "You never been there? What's 'a matter, you scared? Your mommies won't let ya?"

The place was farther downstream than we were allowed to go, and farther than we'd illicitly gone anyway. No telling what was out there, and we could only guess. All the grownups would do was quote the rules as if they were actually written down somewhere and allude to vague bad things that would happen to disobedient little boys. No facts, no real information, just an impatient, "Because I said so, that's why."

This really was "out there" in the finest sense. As far as we knew, civilization was a little island with a few houses on it that was surrounded by endless, howling wilderness. This view was certainly wrong by the 1950s, but it was still widely held, and not just by kids, either. Nature was out there, and it was big and constant. It was about then that the first hints were arising that we humans, with our cars and our industry, were actually changing the world's climate, although it would take the better part of forty years for anyone to get excited about it.

And you could, in fact, go too far. We knew that in family bibles there were accounts of people who were born (usually back in the 1800s) but no records of those people's deaths: just a birth date, a dash and an ominous blank space. So that much was true: you could leave home one day and never be seen or heard from again, just like Grandma said.

We stopped to dig some worms at the edge of the woods because we couldn't be sure there'd be worms where we were going. We were scared, but there were supposed to be these big fish, you see.

This was probably the first time I ever went fishing in a serious way. There were no games, we brought no toy guns, and we didn't stop to chase frogs. We didn't bring any provisions, either, because you had to ask for such things and that would have tipped our hand. This was for real. We were going to bait hooks and catch fish like men. I don't think we even talked much, we just marched off into strange country where the trees got real big and dark and the air had a weird green cast, banking on safety in numbers. I think there were three of us, maybe four: the usual crew.

This was all wrong enough to be deliciously criminal. Even the big kids who had given us the directions were the tough ones my mommy had told me not to associate with. They got into too much trouble, she said, which is why I liked them and studied them. Someday I would grow up, be done with kid's stuff, and get into real trouble myself.

It turned out that the directions were not a joke, which was something you always had to wonder about with the big kids. We walked for a long time (maybe it was miles and miles, or maybe it was hundreds of yards, I can't say for sure) and then we came to the cave we were supposed to be looking for. In front of it was the big, slow pool in the creek, just like they'd said. I think now that the cave was just a cut bank, but it was real dark under there and, as I remember it, the whole woods seemed like a cave.

We baited our hooks, lobbed them into the water and then waited silently. This wasn't much fun, but it was what we knew to be real fishing, which was a man's business and therefore not *supposed* to be fun. Still, there was some kind of grim adult satisfaction to it that we were eager to understand.

The place was spooky: deeply shaded, quiet except for eerie birdsongs that weren't like the pretty ones you heard in town. I think we wondered if maybe we were lost, if only because when you're three feet tall, any place that isn't completely familiar might as well be at the edge of the world. We were too little to have learned that when you're really lost, you know it.

It's hard to say what was in your head when you were five, but I think I had already figured out some things. My mother read me stories, and I liked them, but I knew that real animals didn't have names, didn't talk, and I could see for myself that they didn't wear little hats and shirts.

Okay, but I also knew that other species had lives of their own that were different from mine, but just as respectable. Grandma turned me on to that one day when I stumbled on a snake out

14

in the strawberry patch. It scared me, I froze and started screaming, and Grandma came loping across the yard brandishing a hoe. She didn't know what was after her grandson, but she was going to send it back to its maker in a dozen pieces.

But when she got there and saw what the problem was, she set the hoe down, took me by the shoulders, and said, in her best give-me-your-full-attention voice, "Hush now, you're gonna scare this poor snake to death."

So I knew that some things were real and some things weren't, and that the woods and the creek were real, more and more so the farther you got from home. I think I experienced this as I sat there fishing, half frightened and half bored. I remember that the creek was bigger down there, deeper and too wide to cross. This was total wilderness. It didn't occur to me to wonder where the old tires had come from.

What happened next was: I hooked a sunken log, panicked, hauled back with everything I had, and broke my pole. I say that in the interest of accuracy because that's probably how it was, although there *is* the possibility that I was right in what I assumed at the time, namely that

I had hooked the hugest, nastiest catfish in the world and it had tried to drag me in and kill me. I had seen nothing because the water in the creek was always brown.

Whatever, it was over in a second—my pole was broke, my spirit was wounded, and I wanted to go home. The rest of the guys were ready, too. They may even have been relieved.

We got caught somehow—somebody probably lost his nerve under interrogation and ratted, although it wasn't me—and we got yelled at and swatted. These were remote times, as I

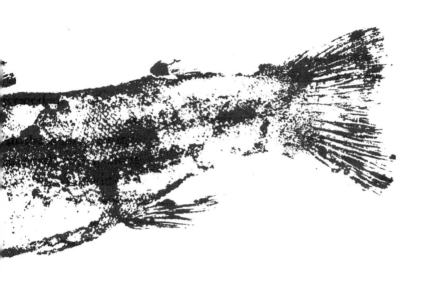

said, and it didn't occur to anyone to say, "Well, at least he's not smoking crack." Going too far into the woods against express orders was serious stuff. You could burn in hell for this kind of thing. Grandma would have to speak to The Lord about it.

I think I was five when all this happened because when I was six I caught polio and things were quite different for a while. But when I got better I already knew all I'd ever know for sure about fishing: that when done properly it is socially unacceptable, and that the farther out there you go the better it gets.

17

THREE

That's probably why I moved out to the Rocky Mountains after college. According to the outdoor magazines of the time, the West was where it was at—big trout, big game, wilderness, elbow room, real tobacco-chewing guides. By then the family had lived in Illinois, Minnesota, and Ohio, but Colorado—where Ike used to go to fish—might as well have been Tibet.

This was in the late sixties, so there was the counter-culture perspective as well. It was said that you could be a righteous subsistence hippie in the West because the neighbors—mostly staunch individualists themselves—tended to let you be, and because you could find a place where there weren't that many neighbors to begin with. That turned out to be true up to a point.

18

The secret spot then was a stretch of small brown-trout stream about twenty miles north of town. It was private, but the two elderly brothers who owned it didn't care if people fished there or not. I mean they honestly didn't care—they hadn't even put up a fence—although they didn't advertise it, either.

Gil Lipp, my first native Colorado friend, took me there in the beginning, and after that we fished it together often. There were industrial-looking irrigation dams and headgates that made fishy pools. You couldn't see the traffic on the highway because of the trees, but sometimes you could hear it. In the fall when the leaves started to come off the cottonwoods, the tower of the Ideal Cement plant would materialize through the higher branches.

It wasn't idyllic, but compared to the Midwest it was downright pristine, and there were lots of trout that weren't all that hard to get on most days. We didn't catch the biggest ones, but we saw them now and then. I learned that this is preferable to not catching the big ones because there aren't any.

For a season or two we had the place pretty much to ourselves and I, at least, learned a lot about fly fishing, technical and otherwise. Even when I couldn't catch the trout, I'd be able just to enjoy what I had in front of me: a cold stream, brown trout, fly rod, the Colorado foothills, and no other people. Except for the cement plant, it was just like in *Field & Stream*.

Of course, the romance of the West tarnishes a little when you live here. For instance, I was told that when President Eisenhower came out to fish, the Division of Wildlife would stock a whole bunch of big, dumb rainbows in his river, knowing that reporters would take photos of Ike holding these things, that the pictures would run in newspapers all over the country, and that the state of Colorado would get a lot of good, free publicity. But what the hell? It's that kind of thinking that made America what it is today. And it's said that when the President and the reporters left, the locals, who'd been hiding in the trees like a pack of coyotes, would come out and catch the fish.

The word eventually got out on the little, secret brown trout stream, and I'm afraid I had something to do with that. I innocently mentioned this place where I was catching a lot of trout to a guy who ran a fly shop. He hadn't heard about it. Odd. I thought the guys who ran fly shops knew all about this stuff. Sometime later I met a stranger on the stream who said that so-and-so down at the such-and-such Angler had told him about the place. Why that possibility hadn't occurred to me I'll never know.

I wasn't mad at this fisherman, you understand. The guy who sniffs out your spot somehow, or falls into it through dumb luck, is nothing more than earnestly alert, and has only done what you did. He was using a fly rod, he was releasing most of his fish, and it was even kind of nice to talk to the guy when it was just him.

In time, other people learned about the place too, and not all through that channel. I like to think I'm not completely to blame—that it probably would have happened anyway. In any case, the stream is still here, you can still get on it, and it still holds brown trout, but the fish are all small and wary now. The big ones I never could catch are gone. I'm a better fisherman now, and if those trout were still there, I might be able to get them. Hell, I *would* get them. I've gotten others just like them.

I guess you never understand the full weight of a moral principle until you've violated it once and seen what happens. The principle pertaining to secret spots goes something like: hide the truck while fishing and keep your mouth shut afterwards. Lie if necessary, even if it means you won't be able to brag.

So you live and learn, and today I am the very model of discretion. I don't know nothin'. Never heard of the place. Sorry, can't help you. I've even been told that I now have a reputation for being closemouthed about fishing spots. I hope so, because if someone is toying with the idea of letting me in on something great, such a reputation could just make the difference.

Last summer, on the annual expedition to Montana, a man I know up there let me fish a stretch of stream that flows through his ranch. That, of course, is all I'm at liberty to say: a man, a stream (probably one you've never heard the name of anyway) on a ranch somewhere in Montana. I think that much is okay. It's a big state. Lots of streams, lots of ranches.

I'd fished this stream the year before, but lower down, on the guy's old spread. He'd bought a new place a few miles up the drainage since then with a slightly longer, and somewhat better, stretch of the same water on it. "I think you'll enjoy it," he'd said over the phone.

We're talking about pieces of property here with price tags in seven figures. One wonders how much the quality of the fishing had to do

with the move, although maybe one doesn't actually ask.

I showed up unexpectedly, and it turned out
that my host was busy that day—some urgent
business having to do with horses—so I fished
alone. That was perfect, even though I would
like to have fished with the guy. He's said to be
quite good.

I was traveling alone anyway and had, in the
last couple of weeks, gotten pretty deeply into
being a kind of self-contained, wandering her-
mit who didn't have much of an itinerary and

who seldom spoke, using only short sentences when it was unavoidable. Every trip develops its own character, and this was the one where large blank spots developed in my facility to process information. For instance, somewhere between Bozeman and Big Timber I passed a road sign that, because of chipped paint, seemed to say, "GAS FOOD LOGIC, NEXT RIGHT" and didn't think anything of it until I'd been back home for a week.

Technically, I was working—researching stories, shooting photos, soaking up local color—although an uninformed observer might have assumed I was on some kind of rambling,

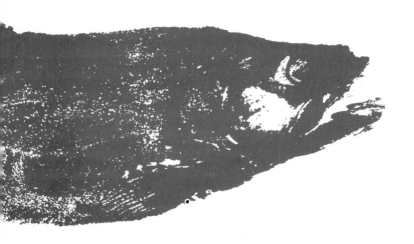

existential vacation. I have to admit that I do now enjoy what I call my "job." There was a time, once, when I thought being a writer would probably be fun. And sure enough, twenty years later, it is.

The man said I'd better get on the water before the day got too hot. This was a blistering August and the fishing had been best in the mornings. He told me where his upper and lower property lines were, where the best stretch of water was, that I should start with a #14 Elk Hair Caddis, and that the last pair of fishermen to work the stream had caught fifteen trout by noon. That was all I needed to know.

The stream was the ideal size for fly fishing: deep and wide enough that it couldn't be crossed just anywhere, but still small enough that you could find a place to cross if it came to that. It was either on the big side of little or vice versa. Anyway, there were lots of trout and no genuinely unreachable spots.

In this stretch there was a sandstone cliff along the far bank and tall cottonwoods on my side, making a lone fisherman feel nicely hidden. This was on a fairly flat section of the shelving, pasture-land valley, so the pocket

water was stretched out into wide, shallow rif-
fles and long, deep, luxurious pools.

The fishing was, let's say, easy. The man had
said, "Fish a caddis fly" so that's what I tied on,
even though there were no rises and no insects
to speak of on the water. I hooked fish in most
of the places that looked right. They were all
browns, healthy, chunky, brightly colored, and
in various sizes.

The trout would roll on the fly confidently.
Some of them moved a good distance for it
without hesitation or apparent second thoughts.
I missed a few strikes, and a few trout ignored
the fly or turned away because I'd dragged it,
but most just ate the caddis pattern and I caught
them without much trouble. I marked the spots
where I'd missed good fish, figuring to rest
them and maybe come back later.

When some big mayflies started coming off I
switched from the caddis fly to a #12 Adams dry
without stopping to catch a bug for an identifica-
tion. It looked like a Green Drake, but it had
become clear that these distinctions wouldn't
matter. The big bug/big fly approach would be
plenty good enough. I caught more fish, then
went back and hooked most of the trout I'd

27

missed before. I began to feel like I was pretty good at this, became confident, tried some fancy casts and managed some of them.

I fished up and down a quarter mile of stream for a couple of hours and managed to lose track of the trout I caught and released right at fifteen, precisely at that point where competitiveness was satisfied, but beyond which it could become unsavory. I had done as well as the last guys—maybe even a little bit better—but who's counting?

That was about it. If it was always this easy I'd be out of business: there'd be no dramas to write about, no great saves or horrible failures, just trout—lots of them, nice fat dumb ones all between ten and fifteen inches—about which you can only say so much.

Once, long ago, this is what it all must have been like, and that sample of the constancy of nature is all you can reasonably ask of a good secret spot. The fish don't have to be enormous, and there don't even have to be as many of them as I caught there that day.

This was going to be the last morning of fishing at the end of a long, solitary road trip. There was a hard drive ahead, and then I would be back where I could be reached by mail and telephone—talking to people at some length again. That would seem strange for a day or two, but it wouldn't be all bad. This good, solid couple of hours on the water—a workmanlike day, but not a fabulous one—seemed just right. If it had been a movie, this would be one of those long parting shots where things are finally back to normal, the music comes up, and the credits roll slowly.

I reported back that I'd done well, and the man asked me if I'd like to stick around for another day because tomorrow the horse business would be taken care of and we could fish together. I explained that I couldn't because I had to go meet my girlfriend, Susan, two states away. I'd been gone for a couple of weeks by then, and she was leaving day after tomorrow for two weeks in Michigan. In the interest of romance, I had promised I'd see her before she left. I think she expected that to be for more than one day, but the day I could still manage would cover it.

Maybe I explained this in more detail than would have been necessary, leaving the impression that I was slightly embarrassed about it, but the man just nodded wisely. "You're doing the right thing," he said.

This is often the way it happens with other people's secret spots. You get on for a day, two if you're lucky, or, if it's on a regular route, maybe once every season. You get to love these places, but you never really get to *know* them. Still, when you get the chance to fish a secret spot, you just go out of conditioned reflex because, based on past experience, you'd proba-bly be a fool not to. There may be conditions— "Don't tell anyone," "Don't bring anyone else back with you," "for Christ's sake, don't *write* about it"—to which you automatically agree.

Just the sound of the words "secret spot" or "private stream" can make your head start to buzz with unlikely expectations. You think: "If it wasn't good, it wouldn't have to be a secret, right?" But at the same time, you try to temper your assumptions because fishing is ninety percent timing, and if you go this once and are let into it like an old friend, then you're just damned lucky. Even if you don't do all that well, you'll at least see something the exact likes of which you've never seen before, and it's best to be satisfied with that. In fact, politeness *requires* you to be satisfied with that. You never want to force your host into saying, "Look, I said they were in there, and they are, but I didn't guarantee we could get 'em, okay?"

There's a little creek in Montana that I'm really starting to like. I've been on it twice now and haven't even begun to crack it, but I know that it has immense possibilities.

Judging from its high water marks, it's a small but hefty stream during normal flows, although I've never fished it in normal flows. What happens is this: In the summer a lot of water is taken out of it for irrigation, so that through the warm months when I've fished it, the stream gets pretty low. Not so low that it's unfishable, just low enough to make it touchy and difficult.

Then, in late summer and fall, the ditches are closed and the stream comes back up. It actu-   31 ally runs higher in October than in July. By fall there's enough water in the stream to float a canoe and, according to the people I've talked to, more locals jump-shoot ducks on it than fish it.

This is a direct tributary of a large river, and there are tales of truly huge trout running up it in the fall. These are usually unconfirmed stories having to do with crocodile-sized brown trout that are seen once—possibly hooked, but not landed—and never seen again.

There's another wrinkle. The stream has the reputation of being at least slightly agriculturally polluted. The word is that the fish, thought healthy themselves, are best not eaten. Consequently, it's a *de facto* catch-and-release fishery, and that, combined with very thin fishing pressure to begin with, lets the trout get rather large. I've never caught a hog myself, and on a day-to-day basis a sixteen-inch trout is considered pretty good, but there are confirmed stories of eight, ten, and even twelve-pound resident fish.

On the last trip I fished the stream with my friend Dave Carty, who owns a piece of land along it and therefore has access. We went out in the evening because the stream is known to go dead through the middles of the summer days—dead enough that you'd swear there wasn't a fish in it—but in the evenings, once the light is off the water, insects hatch and the trout feed.

I'm told that this stream changes character

along its length, as streams tend to do, but where I've fished it it's cut into the floor of a valley. It's a meandering, brushy, often tree-lined strip of riparian habitat running between high banks through pastures, hay meadows, and the odd backyard, all seriously private, of course.

Nothing much was going on when we got there in the afternoon, so we just worked the water. Dave fished a practical nymph and I fished a dry fly. We both caught a few trout, although some of his were larger than any of mine. Dave is primarily a bird hunter, but he's no slouch with the fly rod, and he knows this stream well.

The water in this stretch snakes around a lot and it's jumbled with log jams, bend pools, plunge pools, cut banks, and short runs. There are high, brushy banks along both sides, so you can't see out and no one can see in, either. I've never seen anyone in there except Dave, and, although I'd fished the big river in this valley several times, I had to look at a map before I realized, hey, there's another stream over there.

The fishing here in the summer is sort of painstaking. The water is low, and you need the correct fly, fine leader, good drift, and you can't go splashing around or waving your shadow on the water. Even when it's all working right, you catch a lot more little fish than big ones. When there's a secret spot in the air, the implication is that the fishing will be easy, but it's surprising how often it's not.

There were some thunderstorms building around the valley that day. The sky got dark early and some trout began to rise here and there. We had several hours of fading daylight ahead of us, and Dave said it was beginning look like a promising evening, but of course you can never tell for sure. Then, when the sky clouded over and the air cooled a bit, there were suddenly a few odd caddisflies around, and some pale mayfly spinners were forming up over the water.

I tried the spinner pattern as soon as I saw the flies, but it didn't work—no interest at all from a dozen risers—so I went back to the caddis I'd been using, but left the spinner handy on my drying patch, hoping for the best.

But now that there were some bugs around, the big caddis didn't work, either. After going down two sizes with the same pattern, I started

35

getting some half-hearted strikes and landed a couple of little browns.

Dave and I eventually got separated and I fished alone until past dark. I think the spinners finally started falling on the surface around dusk. I couldn't see them, but I could still see the water and suddenly there were lots more rises, and they were more casual, as if there were now many helpless bugs floating around. The spinner pattern began to work, and it worked better as it got darker. I finally took two good, heavy trout from the tail end of a big bend pool. They were probably browns, although by then there wasn't enough light left to see them clearly.

Then I snagged my fly in something far behind and above me. It must have been a tree (it was too solid and too high for a bush) but I couldn't see anything back there. My tight line just seemed to vanish into the sky.

I broke it off rather than trying to slog back there in the darkness to find it, but in the process I lost almost all of my leader. I laboriously re-tied the thing by the light of a pocket flashlight—carefully aiming it away from the pool with the rising fish in it—and when I was all done, with a fresh fly on, it was pitch dark. I gave my eyes a few minutes to get over the temporary blindness from the flashlight beam, but that wasn't the problem. It had just plain gotten dark and I couldn't see anymore. The sky was clouded over, so there wasn't even starlight to work by. Thunder was rumbling and the still air felt as if any second a cool, damp breeze would come wafting down the creek.

I began to wonder how easy it was going to be to get out of there when the time came. Dave would know his way around in the dark, but there was no telling where Dave was.

In the very last of the light—in that dim metallic sheen that seems to come from the water itself—I'd seen many fish working in the pool in front of me. Some of them were very big, and rising steadily. I couldn't see them now, but I could still hear them: rises that sounded like a moose trying to wade quietly in deep, still water.

I made a few cautious casts in what I figured was the right direction. I wasn't able to see anything and otherwise had no idea what I was doing. All I knew was that tomorrow I'd be fishing somewhere else and I wouldn't be back here again this season. There were some very big trout right over there—I could hear them—and I wanted one. Just one, please. I promise I'll just look at it once with the flashlight and then put it back and leave.

Fishermen, you see, have only two time references. There is now and then there's forever. On one hand there's always tomorrow, the next trout, the next stream, the next season, on and on until you're finally too old and beat up to pull on your waders. On good days, that can seem like an eternity. On the other hand there is *this fish right now*, beyond which there seems to be nothing. And that can seem like an eternity, too.

Just then a bolt of lightning lit up the stream, and it was close, too, because the deafening crack and the blinding light came at almost the same moment. I happened to be looking toward the pool, and in that instant of super-illumination I saw the rings of two dozen rising trout and

38

a hundred mayflies in the air, all frozen in time in a kind of pale, science-fiction electric blue.

Then it was black again, but I could still see the whole scene (if I closed my eyes I could probably still see it now) and then Dave's voice, right at my shoulder, said, "How'd you do? Get any?"

It scared the hell out of me, but I somehow managed not to scream.

S I X

Many of the smaller streams I've been fishing in Montana in recent seasons are private, or at least involve some negotiated access. In theory, you can get on a lot of supposedly private water in Montana by invoking their stream-access law—which hinges on whether the thing is navigable or not—but in practice it's usually best to go ahead and get permission to fish or, as I try to do, hook up

with someone from around there who knows the
ins and outs. This tends to keep you out of
those ugly confrontational scenes where being

technically in the right suddenly becomes
meaningless.

It can be an adventure, and there are days
when said adventure doesn't have much to do
with fish.

The name of one stream up there is not Rat-
tlesnake Creek, but if I were to refer to it that
way now in front of Dave he'd know exactly
which piece of water I was talking about. It's
that quiet little stream somewhere in southern
Montana, the one where the trout are big and
all but uncatchable, the one where you walk

slowly, watch where you're going, stay out of the tall grass, jump at every noise, and otherwise never quite feel comfortable.

I'd been in Montana for a couple of days. Dave and I had been fishing the Gallatin River and we'd been doing well, but, as fishermen will do, we'd started talking about some other places we could go. That's when a certain creek came up.

I'd never heard of it. Dave *had* heard of it—favorable reports, mostly—but had never fished it. Word was it was small, pretty, secluded, very productive, and zealously private. One had to know where it was and how to get on it. Dave did know where it was—sort of—and as for the rest he knew only that it was owned by a rich, reclusive rancher named something like Bull who didn't care for strangers, but did like a drink now and then.

There were fishermen who had been let on the water graciously and others who had been run off in no uncertain terms just for asking, the determining factor apparently being Bull's mood at the moment. And there were those who had fished it once but had never gone back, not because the trout weren't big, but because there were too many rattlesnakes. And these were tough Montana guys, not sissies with nonresident fishing licenses. All in all, it sounded pretty tantalizing.

That evening we went to a party where Dave ran into a couple of friends of his who knew about the creek and claimed to have some kind of unspecified connection with the place. "We can get on it," was all they'd say, and then they'd exchange the kind of knowing look that made me wonder if getting on involved wire cutters. Their names escape me now, but I remember that they were short, clipped, western names: something like Bob and Buck. They may or may not have been cowboys. I can never tell for sure if they're not wearing those hats.

In the course of telling us about the place (it was some of the best fishing they'd ever had), these two eventually got around to saying they'd take us up the next day. They were drunk, happy, and in a generous, party mood. A little fishing tomorrow sounded like a good idea.

Four fishermen on a small creek is two too many, but what are you gonna do?

"You guys aren't too scared of snakes, are ya?" one of the men asked, and then he insisted that we not leave until noon. Seems he was pretty drunk at the moment and planned to boogie 'til he puked. He didn't figure to be con-

scious again until tomorrow noon at the earliest.

Of course tomorrow noon came and went, and then so did twelve-thirty, with Dave and me sitting on the front porch watching the dirt road for the cloud of dust that would indicate the approaching pickup. I remembered a time when AK Best and I were waiting in a fly-shop parking lot for a man who wanted to go to the South Platte River with us. We were supposed to leave at 5:00 A.M. At four minutes after, AK said, "Well, I guess he's not coming," and started the truck. I'm not quite that impatient, but two guys who are half an hour late to go fishing deserve to be left behind, that is, if the expedition can spare them.

"Can you find this place by yourself?" I asked Dave.

"I think so," he said. Then he stared up into the sky for a few seconds and revised his opinion. "Sure. Hell yes I can find it."

"What about permission?"

"All we can do is ask," he said.

Why not? I wasn't sure it was exactly "permission" that these two guys had in mind, anyway.

We did find the creek, miles down the third dirt road we tried, and at first I was unimpressed. It was fast, shallow, not much shade, not much holding water. It looked like it might have a handful of little brookies in it, at best.

"Is this the right one?" I asked.

"I think it gets better upstream," Dave said.

More miles on a smaller dirt road. Then we passed a cattle guard with a sign on it saying, "NO TRESPASSING." At precisely the point where the stream became private it started to look a lot better. There were more overhanging willows, deeper pools, longer runs, mats of aquatic vegetation.

A few more miles up the same road we came to another sign, a big one with red letters on a white field. It said that fishing was by permission only, that permission could be gotten by calling such-and-such a telephone number during certain hours, and that one *should not go up to the ranch to ask to fish.* We read it over carefully several times, as if we were looking for loopholes in the Ten Commandments.

We'd come a long way on unmarked back roads and figured the nearest pay telephone was no less than thirty miles back. So we drove on up. The stories notwithstanding, all the guy could do was say no.

The stream got prettier with every mile, looking more and more like a classic spring creek.

It's not, apparently, but I'm told the water chemistry is similar and it has that same slow-flowing, weedy, buggy, fishy look to it. There were no cars on the road, no fishermen in the water, just a big, wide valley with a brush-lined stream and hay fields lying out in the lazy afternoon sun.

The ranch house, barn, and outbuildings were at the back of the valley, on the last level piece of land a two-hour drive from town on a bad road. This is the kind of place you'd buy if you had all kinds of money and wanted to be left alone. It was a neat, clean, businesslike spread—pretty and intimidating at the same time.

I began to have some serious doubts about this, but I could see that Dave was getting into his glad-handing mode: squeezing the steering wheel in a hearty, friendly way and trying out his innocent grin. No one has ever accused Carty of being shy. He'll walk right up to anyone and ask him for anything, fully expecting to get it. He's never gotten me into anything but marginal trouble this way and he does have more places to hunt and fish than anyone I've ever known. I was glad that Dave and I, our gear and the pickup all looked well-used. This could be one of those places where long-necked, pale people in clean cars wouldn't come off quite right.

When we pulled up to the side of the house, the dogs—a pair of trim yellow labs—did their jobs by barking at us, but otherwise seemed friendly enough. I looked around for one of those small psychotic-looking blue heelers so many ranchers have, but I didn't see one. They call them "heelers" because that's where they like to bite you.

Then Bull himself came out onto the porch, letting the screen door slam behind him. He was a man of some age; a big man whose movements were slow and deliberate.

Carty walked up, shook the man's hand, and launched his pitch: Yes, we'd seen the sign, but we were already all the way up here. We hope we're not intruding, but we'd sure like to do a little fishing. Naturally, we'll release anything we catch.

Dave pointed vaguely down the valley and added, "I live over in town," hoping that would establish him as a kind of neighbor.

Bull looked at Carty and then at me. I stared

across the hood of the truck into his eyes, wondering if he was ripped, unhappy, or a little of both, but some people's eyes are always watery and vague; some people's mouths are always a straight line, no matter what.

"Aw hell," he said, "since you're here, go ahead, but fish back below that old railroad trestle."

I remembered that this wasn't the best-looking water. It was shallower and more open than the luscious-looking stretch above, but later that afternoon, when it got cloudy and cooled off a bit, it would turn out to be plenty good enough.

"Yes sir," we said in unison.

Bull grunted and walked back into the house. The two labs had stopped barking and one of them was standing right in front of me, wagging his tail. He'd brought me a slobbery green tennis ball. I was going to throw it for him, but he wouldn't give it to me.

We got back in the truck and drove downstream toward the trestle. Dave said that when he got rich and bought a place like this he'd let strangers hunt and fish on it any time they asked, to sort of repay the favors so many people had done for him here in the hospitable state of Montana. He got positively sentimental about it.

It occurred to me that Bull had not bothered to mention the snakes.

S E V E N

AK Best and I had returned from a week-long, three-river trip to Colorado's West Slope just in time to hide out at home during the Fourth of July weekend. As we drove east out of the mountains, we passed hundreds of cars and campers going west. We always congratulate each other when we find ourselves going the other way like that, assuming we must be doing something right if we're not part of a crowd. By the time we peeled off of I-70 down a two-lane canyon road, the westbound cars had begun to clot into something resembling a traffic jam. "Poor bastards," AK said.

It had been hot up in the mountains, and it was even hotter down here on the edge of the foothills: 100° or better for days on end. Record-breaking. Again.

This was the second unusually hot, dry summer in as many years and there was a lot of talk, in and out of the media, about global warming caused by the greenhouse effect. This didn't (and still doesn't) look good, but on the water those two fishermen's time references had

kicked in again. In the long run we're changing our climate and our lives will have to change some with it. In the short run, when the weather is hot you fish in the mornings and evenings and hole up in the shade through the middle of the day.

If that sounds like a flippant response to a potentially serious global problem, consider that at least some of the day-to-day solutions could end up being just that simple. If you'll recall, the Surgeon General's answer to increased levels of harmful solar radiation from the depleted ozone layer was, "Wear a straw hat when you go outside."

"That sounds a little simple-minded," I said

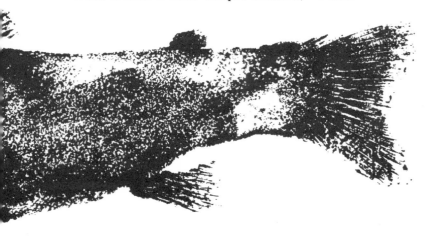

to my friend Ed Engle at the time.

"So what's *your* plan?" he asked.

AK, a professional fly tier, settled into his cool basement to catch up with the frantic orders that come in at that time of year. I sat here in front of a fan in my underwear gazing listlessly at the word processor and listening to the traffic go by. (That's what a writer does on a hot day when he tells you he was "working.")

This was okay for a few days—after the strangeness of a trip it takes a little while to get used to the strangeness of being at home—but then we decided we'd better get back up into the hills, mostly to cool off, but also to kill a few trout. Especially after having released, let's say, sixty or seventy trout each in a week's time, AK and I sometimes like to go kill and eat a few, just to sort of check back in with reality.

They *are* awfully good to eat. Especially the brook trout.

We drove to a little stream in the mountains near here that isn't fished too heavily because it's small and so clogged with willows, sweepers, log jams, and old beaver work that it's all but impossible to get around in. Consequently, it holds some decent trout, an almost even mix of rainbows, browns, and brookies.

The air and the water were nice and cool up there. It was a relief.

We went in at a spot where the creek loops out of the underbrush close to the dirt road. Just around the bend downstream is a sweet, miniature bend-pool/log-jam combination that's best fished by kneeling a rod's length away and feeding a dry fly into the darkest corner of the thing on a foot of leader. I slunk toward the spot, AK wished me luck and headed on downsteam.

The rainbow that lives in there took confidently, but while I was trying to figure out what to do next, he tangled me up in some sticks and broke off.

I found AK downstream at a similar pool, except that this one allowed for a real dry-fly drift if you could make the tight roll cast and the upstream mend just right. He had a ten-inch brown on a willow stick, and while I watched he landed a brookie of about the same size, which he also kept.

53

"I missed a nice one upstream," I said.

"That'll happen," AK replied.

Below there the creek split into channels. I was about ready to catch a fish, so I struggled into the thickest, lowest, most claustrophobic willow tunnel, the one where the fish never see direct sunlight and feed all day long. They don't see many fishermen in there, either.

I fed a #14 Elk Hair Caddis into a flat piece of water with about two feet of headroom and hooked what looked like a twelve-inch brook trout. I played him right to the tip-top guide, couldn't figure out where to go from there, and he got off.

Then I hooked a rainbow who ducked into a Volkswagon-sized log jam and broke me off.

Then a branch flipped my hat off, the hat drifted down through a beautiful little pool with a fish rising in it and spooked him.

Then I came to the head of a somewhat open pool with a dozen good-sized trout in it, all of which flushed like quail when I raised my rod to roll cast.

This is not a secret spot because no one knows it's there. Actually, everybody knows it's there, but it amounts to a secret because it's so hard to fish that very few people try it more than once. But I, of course, am not scared away by that, I told myself. It's good because it's hard, so get into that. Relax. You've caught fish here before.

When I ran into AK again he had five fish— two browns, two brookies, and a fat rainbow— and he was laughing about the big one he'd just missed. There are few things prettier than five bright, wild trout strung up on a freshly cut forked willow stick.

I don't really want to try to describe the rest of the afternoon. Let's just say I failed to catch fish in the worst way—that is, I was hooking them right and left, but couldn't land them. A keeper-sized brown would take my dry fly with heartbreaking confidence, but when I'd set the hook I'd tangle my rod tip in an overhanging branch and the fish would calmly spit the fly out. That kind of thing. As I said, I really don't want to talk about it.

I ran into another friend, Mike Price, who was fishing the only pool in two miles of stream that allowed for real fly casting. He was using a #12 fan-wing Royal Coachman—which he does just to aggravate match-the-hatch types—and he told me he'd released a dozen good trout in the last hour.

"Shoot," he said, "if I'd known you wanted some I'd have kept a few for you."

"I appreciate the thought," I said.

Near dusk, down another brushy side channel, I came to a fair-sized beaver pond, which I fished from the bottom end without getting a strike. It was the first time that day that I'd actually lifted my arm and cast the fly rod. That felt good, but there seemed to be no trout to catch—and no bugs, no rises. Well, maybe all the fish had collected at the head of the pond where a little bit of cold, aerated current comes in. They'll do that on hot days.

I'd climbed the dam and was wading along the edge of the pond toward the inlet when the beaver himself—a big one—surfaced two feet from me and executed a horrendous tail-splash alarm signal. It startled me and I took a sudden step backward—sudden enough that I couldn't extricate my feet from the muck first, so I ended up falling into the pond up to my mustache. I don't know if it was the ice-cold water or fear of a pissed-off, forty-some-pound animal that made my heart seem to stop for a few seconds.

While wringing myself out, it occurred to me that this was the beaver pond I'd fallen through the ice into a couple of winters ago. I'd been rabbit hunting and had tracked one out across a little clearing. The clearing turned out to be a pond covered with rather thin ice, and I fell in. The water was only waist deep, but I had to go in up to my chin to get my snowshoes off so I could get out. I remember getting pretty cold. The rabbit got away.

It was hard to tell with the willows all leafed-out and no snow, but this looked like the place.

The sun had gone behind the mountains, there was a breeze up, and my teeth were chattering. I'd gone up there on this hot July day to catch fish and cool off. I had cooled off nicely and I was beginning to think that was the only good use I'd ever be able to put this pond to.

I threw away the forked willow stick I'd cut hours before and started making my way back to the truck. I wasn't entirely sure where I was, but I knew that if I went north the tangled willows and quaking bogs would end at the road. The road would be familiar, and I could probably tell in which direction the truck was parked.

Ethics and conservation aside, the main prob-

lem with going out to kill a few trout is the vis-
ibility of your failure when you don't succeed.
You meet the boys back at the truck with no
stringer feeling nothing short of naked.

And this is your secret spot, after all, the
place you go to not saying, "Let's go fishing,"
but "Let's *go get some fish.*" It's your ace in the
hole. (Back at the truck AK would say, "You got
skunked? *Here?*" And I'd reply, "It does happen. It could even happen to you sometime.")

At a moment like this you're supposed to say,
"What the hell, you can't always get 'em. But
they're still in there—nice ones, too—and
that's the important thing."

I did say that, and I meant it, but I'd also just
read Joseph Campbell on the spiritual perspective prehistoric hunters brought to their craft.
Skill hardly entered the equation back then—it **58**

was assumed you knew what you were doing. Mostly it was a matter of respect. It's not that you overpowered the game, it was more like the game offered itself to you if you were worthy of it. In return, you thanked the animal and performed whatever rites were necessary to return the creature's spirit to the source so that it could come back again—both for its good and for yours. That's why you could kill and eat things, but the herds and schools never got any smaller. This was the beginning of religion, as Campbell said, and maybe also the beginning of conservationism.

So maybe that's the feeling you have when you get skunked: not so much unlucky as un-*worthy*. I thought maybe I'd gotten too cocky, and the spirits of that pond were saying to me, "Not only do you get no food here, we're gonna give you a good dunking and send you home. This is your second warning. Next time we'll break your leg."

This is the kind of thinking that can go on in the privacy of a secret spot. You can feel humble in front of an audience on public water, but there's nothing spiritual about it.

But, for better or for worse, solitude doesn't last, and by the time I'd crashed out of the willows onto the road I'd already lost it. I wasn't looking forward to explaining why I was all wet (as if it wouldn't be obvious) and I remembered that I'd actually gone so far as to promise someone a fresh brook trout rolled in cracker crumbs and fried in bacon grease.

When I'd last seen Mike he was still fishing that pool, and when I left AK he'd had those five trout, which by now would surely be a limit of eight. I was wet, cold, and slightly lost, but there was still the hope that someone would give me a couple of fish.

E I G H T

Not too long after that I was up at my friend Steve Binder's cabin, paddling his cedar canoe with the wicker seats, catching big trout from the private lake, eating his food, drinking his expensive booze, toasting my feet in front of his stone fireplace, and otherwise wallowing in the good sporting life. One way to get over being skunked on your secret spot is to go to someone else's spot where the fishing is easier and the accommodations are posh. For some reason, my mysticism tends to fade in an atmosphere of high sport, fine tackle, and good whiskey.

Steve probably won't mind if I describe him as one of my rich friends. Gil Lipp introduced me to him and we've fished the private lake together some since then. This is an invitation I do not turn down for any reason.

I guess Gil now qualifies as a rich friend, too. Back when he first took me to that little secret brown trout stream, we were both young, poor, struggling and—as I remember it—idiotically happy. I was a poet and Gil was a novelist. (Or I was a landscaper and Gil was a cab driver, whichever you prefer.) Now Gil—and Binder— belong to those mysterious professions where coats and ties are worn; where everyone is called "Mister"; and where staggering amounts of money are made by talking on telephones, punching computer keys, and, for all I know, burning incense in darkened rooms.

Of course, this business of being rich is all relative. Mr. Lipp does well by any standard, and he owns much fine tackle that he sometimes fishes in exotic waters, but he'll lean up against his black Porsche with the tinted windows, pick a speck of lint from his Italian leather jacket, adjust his custom-made aviator shooting glasses and say, "Well, I'm not what you'd call *wealthy*."

Twenty years ago I hated people like that on

general principles. They were, after all, fascist, anti-populist, military/industrial warmongers. Every last one of 'em. I haven't given up my politics, but I'm a little older now, and it's some of my friends who are rich—or, as we now say,

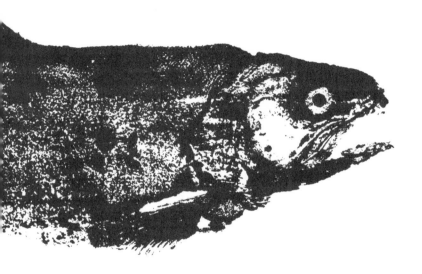

they are WHOFIES (Well-Heeled Older Folks). They're a new crop, and I actually find it kind of comforting to know that some of the guys who are now well-off and even somewhat powerful were, twenty years ago, known around campus as Dr. Feel-good. If nothing else, this allows them a certain perspective.

And I like the way they spend their money,

too, which is exactly how I'd spend it if I had it.

Steve's cabin is one of several on a private trout lake in the Colorado Rockies. The place is nicely off the beaten track—not exactly remote, but far enough back in the bushes that you're surprised to be driving up an ordinary dirt road through the trees only to come upon this no-nonsense locked iron gate.

It's a completely top-notch setup. The lake itself is an "enhanced" natural body of water: a pine- and spruce-lined mountain cirque lake that's been roughly doubled in size with a dam on the downstream end. That work was done in the 1930s and the lake has been managed for quality, members- and guests-only trout fishing ever since, with a relative handful of people involved.

The lake holds rainbows, brookies, and an interesting hatchery golden/rainbow cross: a weird, genetically engineered fish that some like and some don't. These things are an overall golden-yellow color and the eagles and ospreys appreciate them because they're pale on the back and easy to spot.

The lake is stocked periodically and a committee of landowners keeps close track of things. For instance, you can kill trout there, but you have to fill out a report form. This strikes me as a new and especially modern reason for releasing most of the fish you catch: so as to avoid the paperwork.

Steve's cabin was built back in the 1930s. It was in serious disrepair when Steve bought it, but he's restored it now to what I, for one, think of as the archetypal "cabin on the lake": rough log construction, cozy low ceilings, stone fireplace presided over by the mounted head of a large bull elk, rustic furniture, wildlife and sporting art on the walls, quality rods and reels lying around, well-stocked bar, redwood deck directly overlooking the water, modest dock with aluminum rowboat fitted with trolling motor, cedar canoe up on sawhorses, and so on.

Steve and Gil also collect bamboo fly rods—good ones that aren't museum pieces now but probably will be some day. Off the water there's talk of how much some of these things cost and of their investment potential, but on the lake it's all how they feel, how they cast, and how they play fish. One gets the feeling that this investment business is either a holdover from the office or an out-and-out smoke screen.

At some point there'll be a break in the actual fishing and we'll stand out on the dock trying out rods. I've been handed some awfully snazzy pieces of lumber out there—rods by Bob Summers, D. J. Duck, old Leonards, San Francisco Winstons, and such—and Steve has likened it to a wine-tasting. "Well," someone will say, "it's an impertinent little five-weight, but its presumptions are amusing."

Not to be outdone, I asked Steve if he'd like to try my Mike Clark five-weight.

"Jeeze, this is nice," he said. "Who did you say made it?"

"Oh, just a rodmaker I know," I replied.

Once, when I admired Gil's eight-foot D. J. Duck, he said, "Go ahead, go catch a few trout on it." The fishing at the lake is good enough that you can actually go catch a few trout for no other reason than to try out an especially sweet rod.

Of course, you are so careful in this situation that it's almost no fun. I believe that to have lived a full life one should, at least once, have legitimately broken a rod on a fish. To be right, it should be a very good rod and a very big fish, but it should be *your* rod.

This is all very uptown and, yes, I could get used to it, although I probably won't. It is, however, one way to address the problem of the secret fishing spot: find it and buy it, or, failing that, befriend the guy who *did* buy it.

In the course of things, I do get on some excellent private water now and then, and I naturally receive some grief about it from friends who didn't get to go. After some hot-shot trip,

AK will invariably call and ask, "So, are you still talking to your old friends? Are you still putting your pants on one leg at a time?" To which I say, "Have your people call my people and we'll set up a lunch."

But, as I said, when someone invites you, you just go because you'd be a fool not to. You keep your expectations in check, and maybe you do the same thing with your second thoughts, too. It *is* exclusionary—that's why it's so good—but it's also a real way of dropping out of society by going where others don't go because they can't. When I think of it in those terms, it doesn't bother me at all.

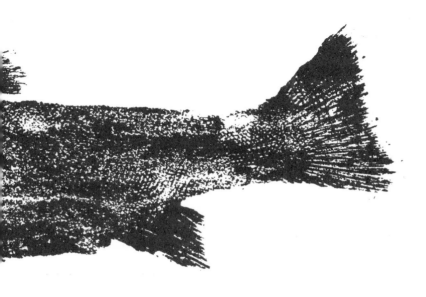

We had everything we needed one early morning last fall: good directions to the lake, complete with prominent landmarks and mileages, and a key to the padlocked gate—not the old wooden gate you come to first, but the iron gate a hundred yards farther along. You can't miss it; it's been freshly painted green. Plus, of course, a pickup load of rods, lines, belly boats, and fly boxes because we didn't know how we'd end up having to fish this thing.

Actually, there were two loads of gear because AK had followed me up there in his own truck. This was a day when AK was not supposed to be out fishing. Seems one of his daughters was about to have another baby and Gramps had promised to be on call. But he'd been on call for two weeks now, which you and I know is way too long for a fanatic to be off the water, especially in the fall when things are quickly slipping away.

Going fishing when you told your wife and daughter you wouldn't is a dangerous gambit, but as a kid AK learned the same thing I did: that if you don't catch hell now and then for being irresponsible and shirking your responsibilities (they don't actually call it being "disobedient" once you're grown up) you're not really a fisherman in the finest sense. So he planned to drive into a nearby town at some point to find a phone and check in. He needed his own truck in case he had to go home.

This was an old manmade lake of the kind that nestles so snugly into the countryside that it seems perfectly natural unless you happen to be looking right at the dike. A couple of generations ago, someone built this thing exactly where a lake should have been: on a shelf between some mountains where, once, a creek too small and shallow to hold trout spread out into a short meadow stretch. These would be senior, untouchable water rights. It's within sight of, but well below, the Continental Divide; low enough to be in the trees, but out of the foothills and into that country where the slopes rise steeply.

It's a shallow, weedy lake with mats of vegetation laced with muskrat trails ringing potholes of open water where teal paddle busily. The bottom must have been hard once, but many seasons' worth of dying and decaying weeds mixed with sediment have covered the bedrock and gravel with swirling black muck that's too soft and clinging to wade through.

The biomass here would be staggering: lots of species of bug, crustacean, and such, and lots of each. It's the kind of lake where trout could grow fat on things like freshwater shrimp, snails, and aquatic beetle larvae. The fish might not be terribly selective feeders, but they'd be grazers instead of risers.

Word was the trout there *were* quite large and,

because the place had been closed and posted for many years, they were also largely undisturbed.

This thing had been, in years gone by, a snazzy private fishing club. There are several old cabins and what must have been a dining hall clustered on the south bank, making the place look like an abandoned settlement. The buildings are empty now, with holes in their roofs and all but a few windows broken. The furniture and stoves have been removed, and rotting doors hanging on one hinge—the kind you could open with one good kick—are still fastened with calcified padlocks. Going slowly to ruin like that, the place looks wilder than if there were no buildings at all. Except for the attentions of occasional fence-climbing poachers, this lake full of big trout had just been left and forgotten.

The deal was, this property backed up against the national park and some high rollers had recently rediscovered it. They were looking to develop it, you know, clog it up with pricey condos, call it something like "Lakeshore Estates in the Pines" and make a pile of money. But then a group connected with the Nature

Conservancy came in and acquired it so as to be able to leave it pretty much as it is. This purchase is part of an ongoing program to try to provide a kind of buffer around the national park to keep the unspoiled habitat from being insulated from the surrounding national forests by a ring of development, so that, for instance, the elk will still be able to migrate out to winter pastures.

That's the stated purpose, and I'm sure it's the real one. I have to say, however, that I know some people in the Nature Conservancy, and none of them would see a lake full of big trout as just an interesting footnote to an ordinary land deal. In fact, it was a friend in the Conservancy who gave AK and me the key and the permission to fish. He said that at some point the land would become a Nature Conservancy preserve or be deeded to the national park, but for the moment at least, it was a fabulous trout pond that no one fished.

We got to the lake early on a cold, drizzly morning, the second Friday in September and the third day into the first big autumn low-pressure front. Driving in that morning we could see, through a break in the clouds, that there was a fresh icing of snow above timber line.

It was gray and gloomy as we walked down to the shore of the lake. The still surface of it disappeared into fog at a range of about fifty yards, but we could still see a few large trout boiling here and there. Some ducks could be heard muttering out on the water and their silhouettes would come in and out of focus as the fog scudded around.

I tied on a plain #14 wet fly and hooked a heavy fish on my second or third cast. It turned out to be a brook trout, a good seventeen inches long and eight inches thick from back to belly. It was a beautiful trout that had grown fat on what would be a whole textbook full of trout food if anyone ever bothered to catalog it.

AK made an appropriate fuss about the big brookie, and then we fished on for an hour without a strike between us. This was okay. Neither of us had fished this lake before, but we'd fished ones like it. Places like this often grow enormous trout. They're usually fat, self-satisfied fish that will happily eat any simple, nondescript fly pattern as long as they don't have to chase it, but there aren't a lot of them in there. Nor is there any particularly logical place to fish because the bug-infested weeds the trout feed 74 in are everywhere. The fish cruise around lazily, occasionally breaking the surface of the water with a dorsal fin, but they never get excited.

By the time I'd landed another fish—a rainbow of about eighteen or nineteen inches—AK had worked his way around to the far side of the lake. I could just make him out through the mist. I know he hooked and lost a big one over there because I could hear him yelling about it. I couldn't make out the words (it sounded like a dog barking across a valley) but the tone was unmistakable.

The early fog had lifted into a drizzle that, in turn, worked its way into a steady rain. Then, around midmorning, the ceiling dropped, the wind picked up, and in the space of a few minutes the lightning began. It rumbled at first, and then there was a crack that made me decide I didn't want to be standing out in the open anymore.

I reeled in and headed for the nearest cabin, glancing over my shoulder to where I'd seen AK last. He was already out of sight, but I knew where he was. He'd be huddled in the lower of two small stands of spruce trees over there, not in the tall one that might attract the lightning. He'd be dry in a green rain slicker and olive-drab chest waders, sitting crosslegged on the leeward side of a tree, looking at nothing, face blank, patiently waiting. Except for the pipe, he'd look like an old moss-covered Buddha.

I sat down on the front stoop of the first cabin I came to, in the dry spot that was still sheltered by what was left of the porch roof. I considered breaking the door down and going inside, but

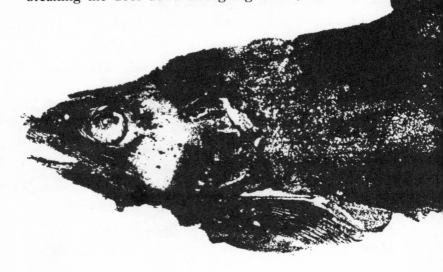

this had once been someone's fishing cabin and, although the guy was probably dead by now, he had locked it up the last time he left and I wasn't going to be the one to kick it open. And 77 anyway, out on the porch I could watch the storm come in. It was raining hard now and the lightning was very close. No time even to count the seconds between the flashes and the explosions you could feel in your diaphragm.

Suddenly it was quite cold—that profound kind of cleansing chill that comes from altitude and thin atmosphere and that feels like a draft blowing under the door from outer space. It felt good, as the beginning of autumn always does to us Germanic types. I like the lush heat of summer well enough, but I can get enough of it.

So I waited the storm out, thinking about how that night I'd build the first fire of the season in the wood stove, and that the house would fill with the nostalgic aromas of a wool sweater and canvas hat drying to wood heat. I started thinking about a place in the house where I wanted to pack some insulation, and about how it was time to spar-varnish the snowshoes.

Then I started thinking about the last thing I'd read on global warming. It was Bill McKibben's depressing magnum opus, *The End of Nature*. This thing outlines—fairly and objectively, as far as I can tell—the profound climatic changes we can expect from the ongoing greenhouse effect, but his real thesis has to do with the relationship between humans and nature.

Once, he says, nature was constant; it was something larger than ourselves that we could count on, even though we didn't completely understand it and sometimes it would scare us or even hurt us. It was like God, or maybe it *was* God. But now that we've changed it (albeit inadvertantly) there is nothing left that we can stand in awe of, no comfort to be found in a natural order. "Soon Thoreau will make no sense," says McKibben, and, "There is no future in loving nature."

There are a few hopeful words in the book, but the basic premise is this: the human race, already in serious spiritual disrepair, will soon fully degenerate into a pitiful, simpering broiling, starving pile of shit.

It's delightful reading.

I've been following this as closely as a layman *can* follow something about which the experts disagree—that is, acting on the single, fair assumption that the guys working for the government are lying. Beyond that, some say, for instance, that the grain belt will get hotter and drier until it becomes a desert, while others claim that the melting of the polar ice will make more water available for evaporation, which will make for more rain, which will make the grain belt wetter and more productive, and with all those clouds maybe it won't get so hot there after all.

The coastal marshes will eventually flood, and they may or may not be replaced by inland marshes. Along the way many coastal cities, including New York, will end up under water. By one account, the only dry land left in the Big Apple twenty to fifty years from now will be the hill in Cloisters Park. An interesting thought to contemplate.

We environmentalists tend to be the most despondent about this, but maybe we should feel good about it. After all, the human race is probably going to get put in its place, and, from an environmental standpoint, that's the only possible solution, as well as being a validation of our position. If nothing else, we'll be able to go around saying, "There, see? We told you so."

Even McKibben—arguably the gloomiest nature lover of all time—says, "This could be the epoch in which people decide at least to go no farther along the path we have been following—when we make not only the necessary technological adjustments to preserve the world from overheating but also the necessary mental adjustments to insure that we will never again put our good ahead of everything else's."

Let us hope, and let's hope too that, if anything, Thoreau will end up making more sense than ever.

Half an hour later, when the rain lifted back into an even drizzle and the lightning had gone away, AK walked over and said he was going down to that little joint we passed to make his phone call.

"I'm going to stay and fish," I said.

"I know," he said, and then added, "you fucker."

Then he drove off to make his call and he never came back.

I got in the belly boat then to try some of the open water I couldn't reach from the bank and found that paddling in the thick weeds was harder than wading. I did manage to catch two more fish, one I'll call twenty-one or twenty-two inches and the next a bit longer, both deep-bodied, and so firm they'd hardly bend. They were enormous rainbows with the dumbest expressions I'd ever seen on fish. They had never been fished for and had no idea what the hell had just happened to them. They'd not only taken the fly confidently and hooked themselves, they'd actually chewed on it, wondering what that hard, sharp thing in the middle was.

It should have been perfect, but I'll admit that sitting in the cold rain for half an hour stewing about global warming had made me a little sad. I consider that an admission because sadness should be shaken off, or at least replaced with something more invigorating, like anger. Sadness is a wimpy, backward-looking emotion. If you want to be anything like happy these days, you have to be happy like a Viking—that is, somewhere between ready and eager for trouble.

Okay, so what about Larry Pogreba's idea?

Just a few days ago I'd been complaining to him about climatic changes and Larry, always the cagey pragmatist, had said, "Okay, we'll keep an eye on it and do something with it."

It's a sketchy plan, but it goes something like this: when the climatic changes and the new weather patterns start to establish themselves, we'll look for that piece of land somewhere—possibly north and uphill from here—where rain will still fall, where trees will grow, where the lakes and rivers will be full of water, and the water will be full of fish. Every climate model allows that there *will* still be places like that.

Maybe it will be in an area that's not all that great now, and so wouldn't be too expensive—a place that a handful of forward-thinking, reasonably self-sufficient outdoors types could buy if they pooled their resources. It could be the ultimate secret fishing spot: the one that doesn't even exist yet.

It's a somewhat wild plan, or maybe it's not a plan at all, but some kind of dream. Whatever it is, it seems to look ahead bravely, and I guess as long as you're wondering how to proceed—rather than whether or not to go on—you're still okay.

The next morning AK called to see how I'd done. I told him it had gotten progressively colder and wetter, and that I'd caught three more trout after he left, all rainbows, each bigger than the one before.

I was soaked, numb, and happy when I landed the last one. The fish ran a few yards and then buried himself in the weeds like a big, scared rabbit. I'd had to wrestle him out of the crap by hand and peel him like a banana.

"He was huge," I said, "enormous."

"How enormous?" AK asked.

"I don't know," I said. "He slopped over the tube of the belly boat on both sides and I couldn't get both hands around him. Seven pounds, maybe. I don't catch that many really big ones, so it's hard to guess."

"Sounds like it was almost as big as my new granddaughter," AK said.

"Yeah, that's right," I said, "congratulations, Grandpa."